Saster,

I am so excited to share this sassy

CW00406054

Write 3 sassy facts about yourself

 I am

 I am

 I am

It is important to remind yourself daily how fabulous and sassy you are!

These are to remind you that you have your own Unique Super Powers aka U.S.P

Now for the fairy godmother dare... do one thing every day that scares you and do it with SAS. xx

Swishes and kisses

JoJo xxxx

Wishes into reality,
fairytales and dreams,
do they really exist ?

Can they be real?

If a fairy godmother jumped in your car as you were pulling off the supermarket carpark and said "grab your pumpkins and set the sat nav for your dream life destination!"

What choice would you make?

A – call security

B – buckle up and start typing in the sat nav

C – admire her tutu and then ask her to tell you more

D – ignore her and just carry on with your day

Whichever of the above you chose ... you just proved that it would be a choice and that it would be YOUR CHOICE how you move forward.

I'm Jojo Smith The sassy not sorry Fairy Godmother and CEO of CreativSAS Ltd, yep I'm jumping in the passenger seat and I'm saying grab your past pumpkins because they are totally your potential, to get you to your dream destination.

Clunk click let's start the trip!!

I want to show you how Personal SAS can save your ASS!

SAS is my pet name for "Self-Awareness Strategy"

CreativSAS is my company that I am beyond proud of and created back in November 2019 just before the whole world changed.

CreativSAS helps discover and develop courage, confidence and self belief through the Cr-Owning of ones USP (Unique Super Power). This in turn becomes your Sassy USP (Unique Selling Point), add this to a sassy branding and business development strategy and the results are you get to create an epic life that serves you by just being you!

This tale could have been very different if it hadn't have been for my OMG moment!! Which now is my proud privilege, passion and purpose to share with anyone that wants to take a leap of faith in life and especially in business?

I have always been 100% committed to whatever I choose to do however it's almost always been in pursuit of approval, acceptance and belonging, this very reason is why My SAS Saved me.

Starting my own business was no different in my commitment, however it was fueled by sheer frustration of the lack of a quality service delivery. As a consumer and seller for lots of companies' honesty and integrity to give good service and value has always been of the highest priority for me.

We all take time away from our nearest and dearest and work hard for our money, therefore the companies we spend that money with, I believe has an obligation to provide fair exchange and integrity.

After years of giving the benefit of the doubt and providing polite feedback which sometimes fell on deaf ears it finally reached breaking point as a seller where I just knew the only way I could make a difference was to be the actual BOSS and be the person responsible to say enough is enough let's just treat people how we would like to be treated.

So, armed with a £100 that my partner gave me, I registered the company name CreativSAS and just like that I was a DIRECTOR …. (I couldn't say that out loud at first, I struggled to own this title - how was I a director?????)

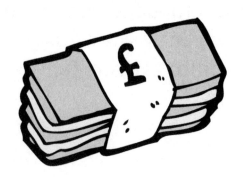

I reached out to a couple of friends in the industry to help me pull a logo together – a logo and some visuals that I could dress my new business with, I was adamant I wanted to be professional and be pleasing to the eye of EVERYONE that came across CreativSAS. I actually said NO PINK Allowed even though Pink was my thing.

A few days later I had a logo that I liked, I ordered some business cards and I was set to go.

The following week I stumbled across a social media post asking for recommendations for motivational speakers, someone fun, vibrant and full of life …. My inner voice squealed that's you Jo have a little look.

I looked and there were several recommendations for the same name ... Dani Wallace, so I got nosey and checked her out.

Here was this larger than life northern soul calling herself The Queen Bee .... she was funny, real, and I was magnetically drawn, so I sent her a cheeky DM because she had in that short moment inspired me to want to know more and made me smile !!

(Who doesn't love to smile .... its infectious .... I'm hoping you just caught the bug reading this bit and you're smiling too).

ANYHOO I digress, I had sent a DM and instantly The Queen Bee replied and had sent an awesome message of encouragement for my new venture. She had shared motivation and connection, instantly some of my faith was restored that it wasn't just me in this world that had this be happy vibe.

Whilst building CreativSAS, I continued to voyeur Dani from a far and every day I felt this person was more on my wave length so when I saw she was going to be local to me in that week I took another leap of faith and sent another cheeky yet polite little DM and asked If I could meet her .... I didn't even know why if I'm honest I was just drawn.

She only blooming said yes and stayed after her meeting had finished which was 9pm to have a cuppa with me at the venue she was at – I drove the 40 minute drive and by the end of that cuppa I had my OMG moment!!

Dani Wallace my level of gratitude for you asking that one question is unmeasurable!!

When I showed Dani my grown up non pink, sensible attempt at branding, with the introduction:

"it's not really me but I know I need to be sensible now" - she asked me what had made me be successful in the past with all my previous clients?

My answer was "My personality, just being lively, bold, fun-loving me with my tilted crown"

OMG !!!

What was I thinking …? Why was I changing myself this is exactly why people had chosen me in the past because I was ME ….? for the first time in my life I saw my own value!!

I made a commitment then and there to take action and to go at this hard and shine the light for others to see their worth!!

From now on I was going to be 100% TuTu pink loving sparkly genuine me!!

Dani recommended I start the branding process with a proper designer and gave me a name.

Let's just say everything turned out ROSIE with my 100% ME Sassy not Sorry new branding so much so that I developed a Creativ collaboration and process that now enables me to bring my signature ballgown branding experience to all my clients.

#SassyNotSorry

That's where the magic really started to happen for me ... The day I created my very own hashtag!!

I remember thinking ... Check me out "I'm not a regular mom I'm a cool Mom – I've got my own hashtag, Wooo Hooo!!"

I wanted EVERYONE to know I was no longer sorry for being ME and that I thought ME was pretty imperfectly awesome and I was going to share that SAS.

The power of a hashtag ... a public affirmation that hopefully would inspire others and could be found at the touch of a button by a total stranger - if I'm totally honest at the time I didn't really know what a hashtag was but I knew that this statement was something that I was wanting to SHOUT LOUD and PROUD, stamp it on a T-Shirt and maybe even brand myself with a tattoo of it! No more dulling down my excitable energy or positivity – sharing is caring and I cared about this message.

I was Taking my positivity power and Cr-OWNING it!!

Let's break Sassy Not Sorry down

Sassy: lively, bold, full of spirit and a lil bit cheeky ...Picture Barbara Windsor, Alison Hammond, Dawn French with a big sprinkle of Stacey Solomon's excitement and Maya Angelou's presence that's the definition of a sassy vibe!!

Not Sorry: Totally Unapologetic for being all the above!!

This claiming my hashtag moment felt like I had been given a big glorious Mr Whippy gold ice cream in one those expensive Italian waffle cones, which by the way
was pink!!! Totally indulgent,
 totally satisfying and left
me fuller than I'd ever felt!!

Finally at the age of 46 I was stepping into my Dorothy shoes and giving myself PERMISSION to be 100% zero Fuchs my passionately positive, wonky crown wearing self!!

This is where my wishes absolutely started to turn into reality, it gave me my super power to create my Sassy Happy Rich Life!!

Aka My fulfilled, loving cheeky not boring or dull and I'm gonna leave a legacy kind of life!! (Rich doesn't always mean money)

Make the choice, and give YOURSELF permission to just be you !!

Reaching my hashtag moment really was a huge shift for me

I now make no secret about my crown being on the wonk in fact I absolutely Own the fact that I am far from perfect, a curvy girl that has no flash qualifications and whose grammar and tech skills are my nemesis yet here I am a published author, with an email subscription list and website that has global traffic!!

boing cartoon eyes moment

#Sassynotsorry!!

Being publicly unapologetic wasn't always the case, for years I wasted hundreds of hours and £s on trying to present myself with a very straight pristine crown - I thought that's how I needed to be to fit in, to be accepted, to be wanted, to be successful and to be secure, when I say presenting myself I mean that literally - because of my curves I was virtually OCD about what I wore and how it all looked, we're talking right from the base layers. My underwear had to match right through to my outer layers and if something was not colour coordinated my mood would dip ….I couldn't have a flaw in the outer packaging for fear of rejection. This even applied to the kids…if their socks didn't match their outfit I was beside myself with anxiety.

How wrong can a girl be   …

All the energy and focus I ploughed into trying to FIT the perfection mould of most of my life situations could power an entire U.S state!! Actually, I have no idea how big a U.S state is but it sounds a lot, so you get my point.

Another area I got the balance misaligned, was my strong moral compass and mantra - a saying that I lived my life by and had consciously instilled this into my kids Jacob and Jessica.

"Treat people how you would like to be treated"

Serving others has always been my thing, treating others how I would like to be treated has always been my thing - just be honest, be kind, be loyal, be considerate and be encouraging.

I always wanted to leave everyone with a feeling of joy and create a memory or experience that was treasured memory worthy.

My definition of treasured memory worthy is giving people an experience or a feeling of being special so they can bank that feeling and have it as a resource when they need it most - to bring them joy, you could say it was a gift of mine to fill up the magic memory bank.

In work or play the attention to personal detail was where my skill always excelled itself... just going that extra mile to create something memorable was not only my joy but it was almost a fix /addiction something I would go in search of in most situations.

My perception was that this gave another person the feeling that they were loved, valued, accepted totally cherished, it was and still is important to me that others feel special.

So here I am treating people how I would like to be treated so that was good right??

WRONG .....

It was good but ... I was missing a crucial element of this mantra....

I wasn't applying it to the relationship I had with myself,

I wasn't treating myself how I deserved to be treated, when I look back now I realise I didn't see my own worth or love myself enough to cherish myself - it didn't even occur to me to be kind to myself and learn to love me.

Filling everyone else's magic memory bank was something I was born to do and I love it still ... it's just so sad that I never stopped or listened to myself to treat myself with the same high regard ... yes I got joy from What I did and when there was appreciation I also got my validation stamps which in hindsight was probably the richer payment that I needed .. being valid and belonging somewhere is actually what I was in search of!!

What I didn't know then was I HAD THE POWER to cement my own value and self-worth which actually would be the key to so much more – if only I had known that I just needed to accept me first.

Yep just Accept myself warts and all.... hmmm that sounds simple enough......
lol!

Let's face it, if it was as easy as it sounds, we would all be living Sassy Happy Rich Lives.

It's one of the biggest hurdles we as humans face especially as we get older and our minds are shaped by our past. We listen to our mind monkeys and base our courage, confidence, self-belief and acceptance on mainly the negative narrative of our past personal experiences, it's OUTRAGEOUS that our focus mainly goes to what we can't do rather than what we can – imagine if we listened more to the positives from our past , all the good stuff ….how UNSTOPPABLE could we be !!

I have my own mind monkey vigilantes now called The Finkin Fairies -They are sassy little f*%ers that kick ass with SAS. Everytime self-doubt or worry knocks my door, they are waiting in their little sassy leather jackets with a portfolio of powerful positive reminders – like Sassy security Tinkerbelle's on a nightclub door.

Powerful Positive Reminders or as I call them … My Positive Pumpkins !!

As a fairy godmother, pumpkins are part of the job and feature heavily in everyday life but what actually is a pumpkin and how can a pumpkin be relevant or positive to you?

Remember that sassy power called CHOICE….. this is where you get to CHOOSE what your pumpkin definition is -

Is it a carved scary face of horror staring back at you, causing fear?

Is it a Seasonal subject that has a lot of negative space inside that you just don't know what to do with?

OR

Is it a well-rounded fruit with a thick rind , the flesh of which can be oh so sweet or savoury – totally adaptable?

Could it even be YOUR fairytale carriage in disguise?

Imagine if Pumpkin was an affectionate reassuring reframing term for your past self?

For me I decided to make a very deliberate choice a few years back. That my Scary negative Pumpkins from the past would be my Powerful Positive Reminders of what I had overcome, these would now transform into my potential.

So grab your pumpkins and keep reading as this is where your past adversity, hardship, trauma or anxieties can be reframed into your personal potential.

This is what I call my SAS journey – this is the road I travelled that lead me to my now ever evolving Sassier Happier Successful Self.

In my instance, we need to go back to childhood to truly understand why acceptance and belonging was so important to me and why it has clouded my self-belief and self-worth in later life.

This is my "R" story because I'm sure you will tilt your head and say Arhhhh at some point whilst reading it lol xx

At 18 months old I was placed in foster care as an unwritten adoption case due to my birth mum not wanting or allowing it to be an official adoption as she had already had one child adopted and she didn't want to lose complete contact with me – Mum (Ann) had M.S-Multiple Sclerosis and limitations that meant she couldn't take care of me, she desperately wanted to but just physically could not.

I was truly blessed and placed with a RICH family, not money rich but love, nurture and support rich. I was gifted a very blessed life, I was gifted a proper FAMILY, we're talking Mum, Dad, big brother and a fully extended loads of cousins kind of family,very happy days and memories.

Fast forward to the age of 6 and out of the blue my birth mum's health improved rapidly and it was decided by social services that mum was well enough to have me back – this was a huge shock and had a big ripple effect in my big gifted family - My life and support structure changed on a colossal scale …. now it was just me and my mum in a two bedroom flat on a not so great estate.

My secure family life was gone and I had to grow up fast, Mum still had a lot of limitations so I had to be quite self-sufficient – walking to school by Spaghetti Junction – Birmingham UK on my own at 6 yrs old kind of self-sufficient. I would have to go to the shop on my own – make my own entertainment – one of my biggest memories is asking my teacher if I could have the school paper display Christmas tree off the wall as we hadn't got one . I rapidly adapted and never questioned why I was there -I just accepted it and made the most out of what I had.

Fast forward a year and one evening my Mum becomes paralyzed literally sat in a chair can't move instantly paralysed, I have to call an ambulance, and stay at a random neighbours house overnight.

The following day I am placed in a local institutional children's care facility (aka a children's home). Overnight my world changed again and I found myself in an environment that was scary, lonely and I just didn't feel I belonged there.

On arrival at Birkdale House I was issued with a locker, 5 pairs of pants, 5 pairs of socks and plastic sheet for my bed in a dormitory of 8-12 beds. I remember feeling mortified with the plastic sheet, I was a big girl and I did not wet the bed!! I have lots of memories from this time most of them leave me feeling just sad that I was alone to deal with them and didn't have that hand to slip my hand into to hold and feel safe and secure.

Almost 2 years later and purely by accident My Rich Mum Dad And Brother now plus another brother find out I am back in the care system and after several months of home visits I'm placed back where I started in the loving grasp of my extended gifted family ....

Told ya ....I know you just did it ... did you just tilt your head and say Arhhh ??? lol xxx

I call it my R story because for me it's the absolute core to my Personal SAS (Self Awareness Strategy) philosophy!!

R For Resilience,

R For Reframing

R For Resourcefulness

All these are my past pumpkins that are now 100% my pure personal potential and power bank for my Self-belief.

I came through all of that and more in later life and now I CHOOSE to focus on the positives strengths that these situations brought out in me. I CHOSE to become Self Aware.

Becoming self-aware is a type of self-security system – its understanding what makes us tick and where our vulnerabilities are, knowing our strengths and triggers so we can adapt accordingly when needed. It enabled me to love, trust and believe in myself.

Note - it's a system that requires regular updates because it's always in use. It requires ConSAStency.

Everyday life requires us to use either Courage Confidence Or Self-Belief whether that be in our work, home life or relationships.

We all make wishes for something we want or dream about however some of us get those wishes and some of us don't.

The simple reason for the above is some of us Get in Our Own Way and some of us don't!!

This is a Big reason for not achieving your wishes.

My philosophy is that YOU can create your wishes into reality with strategy – because YOU are responsible for how YOU show up and the action YOU decide to take.

·YOU decide if you believe that you can truly grant your own wishes into reality.

·YOU decide if you Make the wish

·YOU decide how to respond to the The Worry Alarm and The What if self-doubt.

·YOU decide if you Will Take Action to plan The Way to your Wish

For the past 15 months, I have made it my business to spread SAS - to work on myself and with others to become more Sassy Not Sorry and self-aware, to have a strategy in place to manage and recognize when the self-doubt appears.

I have created The Wish Wheel approach it's a strategy that I follow every time I make a wish and guess what?

…. The wish becomes reality

… this shizzle works!!

How do I know it works …because in 15 months my wishes keep coming true. Just one example: 8 months in to my business I made a wish to deliver a one to many workshop to help people Cr-OWN their Courage and Confidence and Self-belief, I was intentional, I took action, I overcame my what ifs and worry alarm and FAB U SAS launched in January 2021- the first of what I plan to be a series of "Cr-OWNING U workshops.

The survey results from the workshop made me grab my own face with excitement – Each and every person had given it an overall 10 out 10 rating. The scores for personal improvement in Self-belief, Courage and Confidence was now scoring in the high 9's coming from as little as 3s …..

My SAS (Self Awareness Strategy) was actually saving ASS, putting my techniques and strategy into practice is now proven to move you forward, not just in me but in others too.

My Company CreativSAS has evolved into something I am excitably proud of, it's a good job because being The Business Development and Branding Fairy godmother it wouldn't be a good advert if my business wasn't developed and if the branding didn't truly align to its founder.

MY promise to you is If you develop Self Awareness, your business and life will develop, the two work in tandem, Showing up and taking action as YOU will attract the right people into your life .

You Must Understand Your Crown Before You Can Sit On Your Throne ....

I made a wish to be my own boss so I could serve with the integrity that I felt was sometimes missing in client service delivery.

I made it happen CreativSAS sees the following in just 15months:

·Over 11 new brands developed with what I call "Ballgown Branding" through creative collaboration

·Creative license given with a huge global corporate brand on several projects including a staff recognition scheme

· Creative Consultancy Clients within the education sector

· A successful personal development workshop delivered and due to launch again this year

· Several individual creative direction clients where I work with them to discover and develop their U.S.P (Unique Super Power)

· Some seriously Sassy Creative stuff that just makes me smile including my own range of notebooks available on Amazon

· Several Expert Speaking appointments to spread SAS and the Ballgown Branding ethos
Clients that include, celebrity status, online influencers and a fabulous Olympic medalist

The Really Big Wish for me was this one:

I made a wish to be a motivational inspirational speaker when I saw how it could inspire, encourage, and empower courage, confidence and self-belief.

In the past year, I have spoken in several groups and on several podcasts and this month I recently opened the second day at an online LIVE event that is out there for an international audience …….eeeeeek!!!

This wish is now my reality and I got there with SAS!!

I spent years getting in my own way and adapting myself to fit situations so I would belong ….

The irony is that the minute I accepted myself and reframed and retrained all my negative truths with my positive truths and truly
Cr-owned my bespoke uniqueness was the moment I realized that.

BESPOKE IS WHERE I TRULY BELONG!!

JUST BEING ME IS POWERFUL AND ENOUGH!!

Bespoke is where we all belong it's your Unique Superpowers that are your unique selling points, it's learning to Cr-OWN them that is key to your Sassy Happy Rich Life!!

Back in that children's home, I wished for a fairy godmother to hold my hand and guide me through ......

The Happy Sassy Ending is .....

I BECAME HER and you can too!

#sassynotsorry

Useful links and where to find your fairy godmother

 https://www.creativsas.co.uk/

 https://www.facebook.com/CreativSAS

 https://www.instagram.com/creativsas/

Come and hang out with me and a beautiful bunch of SASters.
in The Happy Sassy and Successful SAS
https://www.facebook.com/groups/thehappysas

Grab my FREEBIE - 22 Steps to Happy Sassy & Successful
https://www.subscribepage.com/welcome-to-a-happier

Printed in Great Britain
by Amazon

83245674R00031